*K*nitted Prayer Shawls™

Foreword

FULL-OF-PRAYER SHAWLS

Knitters as a group are always willing to share their talent with others, but occasions do arise when giving someone a knitted gift is just not enough. Those occasions, whether they are joyous or sad, call for something more, something that requires the personal involvement of the knitter.

For that reason, many churches have started prayer shawl ministries. When a knitter is stitching a prayer shawl, she petitions God with every stitch she makes on behalf of the person who will receive the shawl.

If the knitter knows the recipient of the shawl, she can pray specifically for the recipient's needs, for the concerns of the family and friends, and for the circumstances. In some cases, however, the knitter does not know who will receive the shawl. Then she will simply petition God on behalf of the unknown recipient to provide comfort, fill a need, or bless the person. When the prayer shawl is presented to a person, prayers are given again, invoking God's blessing on the recipient and praying more specifically for their needs.

WHO CAN KNIT A PRAYER SHAWL?

Anyone can knit a prayer shawl. If you are a beginning knitter and your only project so far has been a scarf, think of the shawl as a very large scarf. Measure the width and length of a scarf you enjoyed making to help you to decide how many times you need to multiply the number of stitches to cast on. In most cases, you will need to double the length of your scarf to create a shawl.

PRAYING AS YOU ARE KNITTING

Once you begin to stitch the shawl, think about the recipient and how much you love and care for him or her. Give thanks that you have been blessed with the talent to make a gift that will give another person comfort and joy.

After you have given thanks, think of the person for whom you are making the shawl. Let the love you feel for him or her fill your heart and mind; then begin to pray for that person. With each stitch you make, continue to pray for the needs of that person and ask God to bless him or her.

GIVING A KNITTED PRAYER SHAWL

Many churches with prayer shawl ministries have a special time for presenting these gifts of love to the recipients. Whether you are part of a special prayer shawl group or are making a shawl on your own to give to someone in need, consider this time of presentation as an opportunity to give a blessing or say a prayer verbally with the recipient.

To help you with this presentation, we've added a special section of prayers and blessings, and have also listed prayers with each item. Select the prayer or blessing that will bring the most comfort and joy to the person.

Prayers and Blessings

NEW BIRTH

Help this baby to be healthy and strong.

Bless this child. Help him/her to grow and thrive in a way that would honor his/her parents and his/her God. Help him/her to know love and to share his/her love with those around him/her.

Heavenly Father, may this child live a life of love and share that love with those around him/her. Help him/her to do what is right and just and fair. Grant that this child will learn responsibility, for each one should carry his own load.

MARRIAGE

As these two individuals join their lives together, I ask that You guide them into oneness of life as husband and wife, with each one looking at the other as chosen by God. Wrap them in Your arms in times of distress and give them the courage to say, "I'm sorry," when they are wrong. May they look to You for comfort, strength and wisdom.

Bless this couple as they celebrate their marriage. May they continue to realize the importance of family and fun times. Help their love for each other to grow deeper to sustain them in times of difficulty.

SORROW

May the recipient of this shawl find peace during this time of sorrow as he/she wraps himself/herself in Your love and in this knitted prayer shawl.

Lord, You are the great comforter. Surround these dear ones with loving arms as they grieve. Give them strength and peace to carry on, resting in Your sustaining power.

ILLNESS OR STRESS

Lord, sometimes stress overwhelms us until it seems we have no place to turn. Open Your arms as we flee to You. Be our tower of strength. Help us to live one day at a time with Your wisdom and in Your peace.

We come to You, Lord God, healer of every ill, and ask for a release from pain for all the hurts that have been endured and for the gift of healing. Touch this one and bring peace and healing to his/her body and soul.

When the storms of life have tossed us to and fro, may we find a refuge in You, Lord. Plant a seed of hope and water it, that it may grow until hope will fill our entire being.

PRAYER OF THANKFULNESS

Thank You for blessing me with the ability to knit. Thank You for the joy, peace and blessing it brings into my life. It is a gift that has brought me countless hours of pleasure and enjoyment. Father, I return this gift to You. Use this talent to serve Your purpose in the world. Bless each item I knit so that it radiates Your love to the person who will receive it.

HOUSE OF WHITE BIRCHES, BERNE, INDIANA 46711

O God,

You are the God of the impossible. I ask for healing and for hope for the future.

Help _____ to lean on Your strength. Give him/her Your peace.

Amen.

Pocket Shawl

SKILL LEVEL

EASY

SIZE
Approx 20 x 60 inches

MATERIALS
- Plymouth Encored Worsted 75 percent acrylic/25 percent wool worsted weight yarn (200 yds/100g per ball): 5 balls lilac #233
- Size 8 (5mm) knitting needles or size needed to obtain gauge
- Tapestry needle

GAUGE
16 sts = 4 inches/10cm in St st
To save time, take time to check gauge.

INSTRUCTIONS
Cast on 83 sts.

Lower border
Knit 5 rows.

Body
Row 1 (RS): Knit.

Row 2: K4, purl to last 4 sts, k4.

Row 3: Knit.

Row 4: K7, *p1, k3; rep from * to last 4 sts, k4.

Rep Rows 1–4 until piece measures approx 59 inches, ending with a Row 3.

Upper border
Knit 5 rows.

Bind off.

Pocket
Make 2

Cast on 32 sts.

Work in garter st until piece measures 8 inches.

Bind off.

FINISHING
Sew a pocket to each end of shawl, centered with lower edge of pocket approx 3 inches from bottom edge. ■

Dear God,

Come and walk beside _____. Help her to lean on Your everlasting arms, to draw strength and hope for the future. Give her the comfort she needs to face the days and hours ahead.

Amen.

Lace Shawl

SKILL LEVEL

INTERMEDIATE

SIZE

Approx 23 inches across lower edge x 60 inches across top edge x 31 inches long

MATERIALS

- Plymouth Encored Worsted 75 percent acrylic/25 percent wool worsted weight yarn (200 yds/100g per ball): 5 balls aqua #801
- Size 7 (4.5mm) 29-inch circular knitting needle or size needed to obtain gauge

GAUGE

18 sts = 4 inches/10cm in St st
To save time, take time to check gauge.

SPECIAL TECHNIQUE

Cable Cast On: *Insert RH needle between the last 2 sts on the LH needle. Knit a st and place it on the LH needle; rep from * for desired number of sts.

PATTERN NOTE

Circular needle is used to accommodate large number of sts. Do not join; work back and forth in rows.

INSTRUCTIONS

Beg at neck edge, cast on 240 sts.

Rows 1–4: Purl.

Continued on page 12.

Lord God,

Grant _____ the wisdom, humility and patience that is needed as he faces this difficult situation. May he always be strong and courageous in his character and in his actions. Amen.

Woven Shawl

SKILL LEVEL

EASY

SIZE

Approx 30 x 72 inches

MATERIALS

- Plymouth Encored Worsted 75 percent acrylic/25 percent wool worsted weight yarn (200 yds/100g per ball): 9 balls country blue #515
- Size 8 (5mm) 24-inch circular knitting needle or size needed to obtain gauge

GAUGE

16 sts = 4 inches/10cm in St st
To save time, take time to check gauge.

PATTERN NOTE

Circular needle is used to accommodate large number of sts. Do not join; work back and forth in rows.

INSTRUCTIONS

Cast on 121 sts.

Row 1 (RS): Knit.

Row 2: Purl.

Row 3: *K3, p7, k2; rep from * to last st, k1.

Row 4: *P3, k7, p2; rep from * to last st, p1.

Rows 5–8: Rep Rows 1–4.

Row 9: Knit.

Row 10: Purl.

Row 11: *P4, k5, p3; rep from * to last st, p1.

Row 12: *K4, p5, k3; rep from * to last st, k1.

Rows 13–16: Rep Rows 9–12.

Rep Rows 1–16 until piece measures approx 72 inches, ending with a Row 8 or 16.

Bind off knitwise.

Edging

With RS facing, pick up and knit 300 sts evenly spaced along 1 long edge.

Row 1 (WS): Knit.

Row 2 (RS): Purl.

Bind off knitwise.

Rep along opposite long edge. ■

HOUSE OF WHITE BIRCHES, BERNE, INDIANA 46711 DRGNETWORK.COM

Garter Point Shawl

SKILL LEVEL

EASY

SIZE

Approx 23 x 68 inches

MATERIALS

- Plymouth Encored Worsted 75 percent acrylic/25 percent wool worsted weight yarn (200 yds/100g per ball): 7 balls deep rose #180
- Size 8 (5mm) straight and 36-inch circular knitting needles or size needed to obtain gauge
- Stitch markers

GAUGE

16 sts = 4 inches/10cm in St st
To save time, take time to check gauge.

PATTERN NOTE

Circular needle is used to accommodate large number of sts. Do not join; work back and forth in rows.

INSTRUCTIONS

Triangle Border
With straight needles, cast on 2 sts.

Row 1 (RS): Knit.

Row 2: Knit in front and back of first st, knit across.

Rows 3–16: [Rep Rows 1 and 2] 7 times. (10 sts)

Row 17: Knit.

Row 18: K2tog, knit across.

Rows 19–32: [Rep Rows 17 and 18] 7 times. (2 sts)

[Rep Rows 1–32] 24 times. (25 triangles)

Bind off.

Body
With circular needle, pick up and knit 16 sts along the long edge of each of the first 5 triangles (80 sts), place marker on needle; pick up and knit 16 sts along the long edge of each of the next 15 triangles (240 sts), place marker; pick up and knit 16 sts along the long edge of each of the last 5 triangles (80 sts). (400 sts)

Row 1: Knit.

Row 2: Knit to first marker, sl marker, k2tog, knit to next marker, sl marker, k2tog, knit across.

Rep Row 2 until 1 st rem before first marker and after last marker.

Bind off all sts. ∎

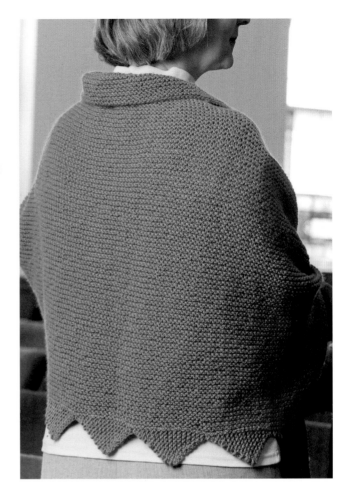

Lace Shawl
Continued from page 7.

Row 5: P3, p2tog, *yo, k2tog; rep from * to last 5 sts, p2tog-tbl, p3.

Row 6: Purl.

Rows 7–10: [Rep Rows 5 and 6] twice.

[Rep Rows 1–10] 24 times. (90 sts)

Rep Rows 1–4.

Bind off knitwise.

I-cord edging
With RS facing, pick up and knit 240 sts along cast-on edge, then using Cable Cast On, cast on 4 sts. *K3, ssk, do not turn, sl 4 sts from RH needle

to LH needle, bring yarn across back of work; rep from * until all picked up sts have been worked and 4 sts rem.

Bind off. ∎

Lord,

You are the giver of life. Thank You for this new life, this little one who will be loved and cared for in this home. Bless this family abundantly.

Amen.

Cabled Shawl

SKILL LEVEL

INTERMEDIATE

SIZE

Approx 21 x 60 inches (excluding tassels)

MATERIALS

- Plymouth Encored Worsted 75 percent acrylic/25 percent wool worsted weight yarn (200 yds/100g per ball): 6 balls sage #451
- Size 7 (4.5mm) 32-inch circular knitting needle or size needed to obtain gauge
- Cable needle
- 9-inch length of cardboard (for tassels)

GAUGE

18 sts = 4 inches/10cm in St st
To save time, take time to check gauge.

SPECIAL ABBREVIATION

C4L (Cable 4 Left): Sl next 2 sts to cn and hold in front of work, k2, k2 from cn.

PATTERN NOTE

Circular needle is used to accommodate large number of sts. Do not join; work back and forth in rows.

INSTRUCTIONS

Cast on 104 sts.

Row 1 (RS): K1, p1, k2, p1, *k4, p1, k2, [p1, k1] 3 times, k1, p1; rep from * to last 9 sts, k4, p1, k2, p1, k1.

Row 2: [K1, p1] twice, k1, *p4, k1, [p1, k1] 5 times; rep from * to last 9 sts, p4, k1, [p1, k1] twice.

Row 3: K4, p1, *C4L, p1, k9, p1; rep from * to last 9 sts, C4L, p1, k4.

Row 4: P4, k1, *p4, k1, p9, k1; rep from * to last 9 sts, p4, k1, p4.

Rows 5 and 6: Rep Rows 1 and 2.

Row 7: K4, p1, *k4, p1, k9, p1; rep from * to last 9 sts, k4, p1, k4.

Row 8: Rep Row 4.

Row 9: K1, p1, k2, p1, *C4L, p1, k2, [p1, k1] 3 times, k1, p1; rep from * to last 9 sts, C4L, p1, k2, p1, k1.

Row 10: Rep Row 2.

Row 11: Rep Row 7.

Row 12: Rep Row 4.

Rep Rows 1–12 until piece measures approx 60 inches.

Bind off all sts.

Side edging

With RS facing, pick up and knit 285 sts evenly spaced along 1 long edge of shawl.

Row 1 (WS): K1, *p1, k1; rep from * across.

Rows 2 and 3: Rep Row 1.

Bind off knitwise.

Rep along opposite long edge.

TASSEL
Make 14

Wind yarn around 9-inch length of cardboard. Cut across 1 end. Tie 1 length of yarn around center of 20-strand group, leaving ends long to attach to shawl. Wrap and tie another length of yarn 1 inch from the fold. With long ends attach tassels to each end of shawl at base of cables. Trim tassel ends even. ■

Metric Conversion Chart

INCHES INTO MILLIMETERS & CENTIMETERS (Rounded off slightly)

inches	mm	cm	inches	cm	inches	cm	inches	cm
1/8	3	0.3	5	12.5	21	53.5	38	96.5
1/4	6	0.6	5 1/2	14	22	56	39	99
3/8	10	1	6	15	23	58.5	40	101.5
1/2	13	1.3	7	18	24	61	41	104
5/8	15	1.5	8	20.5	25	63.5	42	106.5
3/4	20	2	9	23	26	66	43	109
7/8	22	2.2	10	25.5	27	68.5	44	112
1	25	2.5	11	28	28	71	45	114.5
1 1/4	32	3.2	12	30.5	29	73.5	46	117
1 1/2	38	3.8	13	33	30	76	47	119.5
1 3/4	45	4.5	14	35.5	31	79	48	122
2	50	5	15	38	32	81.5	49	124.5
2 1/2	65	6.5	16	40.5	33	84	50	127
3	75	7.5	17	43	34	86.5		
3 1/2	90	9	18	46	35	89		
4	100	10	19	48.5	36	91.5		
4 1/2	115	11.5	20	51	37	94		

KNITTING NEEDLES CONVERSION CHART

U.S.	0	1	2	3	4	5	6	7	8	9	10	10 1/2	11	13	15
Metric(mm)	2	2 1/4	2 3/4	3 1/4	3 1/2	3 3/4	4	4 1/2	5	5 1/2	6	6 1/2	8	9	10

Standard Abbreviations

[ ] work instructions within brackets as many times as directed

( ) work instructions within parentheses in the place directed

** repeat instructions following the asterisks as directed

* repeat instructions following the single asterisk as directed

" inch(es)

approx approximately

beg begin/beginning

CC contrasting color

ch chain stitch

cm centimeter(s)

cn cable needle

dec decrease/decreases/ decreasing

dpn(s) double-pointed needle(s)

g gram

inc increase/increases/ increasing

k knit

k2tog knit 2 stitches together

LH left hand

lp(s) loop(s)

m meter(s)

M1 make one stitch

MC main color

mm millimeter(s)

oz ounce(s)

p purl

pat(s) pattern(s)

p2tog purl 2 stitches together

psso pass slipped stitch over

p2sso pass 2 slipped stitches over

rem remain/remaining

rep repeat(s)

rev St st reverse stockinette stitch

RH right hand

rnd(s) rounds

RS right side

skp slip, knit, pass stitch over—one stitch decreased

sk2p slip 1, knit 2 together, pass slip stitch over the knit 2 together—2 stitches have been decreased

sl slip

sl 1k slip 1 knitwise

sl 1p slip 1 purlwise

sl st slip stitch(es)

ssk slip, slip, knit these 2 stitches together—a decrease

st(s) stitch(es)

St st stockinette stitch/ stocking stitch

tbl through back loop(s)

tog together

WS wrong side

wyib with yarn in back

wyif with yarn in front

yd(s) yard(s)

yfwd yarn forward

yo yarn over

Skill Levels

BEGINNER

Projects for first-time knitters using basic knit and purl stitches. Minimal shaping.

EASY

Projects using basic stitches, repetitive stitch patterns, simple color changes and simple shaping and finishing.

INTERMEDIATE

Projects with a variety of stitches, such as basic cables and lace, simple intarsia, double-pointed needles and knitting in the round needle techniques, mid-level shaping and finishing.

EXPERIENCED

Projects using advanced techniques and stitches, such as short rows, Fair Isle, more intricate intarsia, cables, lace patterns and numerous color changes.

Standard Yarn Weight System

Categories of yarn, gauge ranges, and recommended needle sizes

Yarn Weight Symbol & Category Names	1 SUPER FINE	2 FINE	3 LIGHT	4 MEDIUM	5 BULKY	6 SUPER BULKY
Type of Yarns in Category	Sock, Fingering, Baby	Sport, Baby	DK, Light Worsted	Worsted, Afghan, Aran	Chunky, Craft, Rug	Bulky, Roving
Knit Gauge* Ranges in Stockinette Stitch to 4 inches	21–32 sts	23–26 sts	21–24 sts	16–20 sts	12–15 sts	6–11 sts
Recommended Needle in Metric Size Range	2.25–3.25mm	3.25–3.75mm	3.75–4.5mm	4.5–5.5mm	5.5–8mm	8mm
Recommended Needle U.S. Size Range	1 to 3	3 to 5	5 to 7	7 to 9	9 to 11	11 and larger

* GUIDELINES ONLY: The above reflect the most commonly used gauges and needle sizes for specific yarn categories.

E-mail: Customer_Service@whitebirches.com

HOUSE OF WHITE BIRCHES PUBLISHERS SINCE 1947

Knitted Prayer Shawls is published by DRG, 306 East Parr Road, Berne, IN 46711, telephone (260) 589-4000. Printed in USA. Copyright © 2008 DRG. All rights reserved. This publication may not be reproduced in part or in whole without written permission from the publisher.

RETAIL STORES: If you would like to carry this pattern book or any other DRG publications, call the Wholesale Department at Annie's Attic to set up a direct account: (903) 636-4303. Also, request a complete listing of publications available from DRG.

Every effort has been made to ensure that the instructions in this pattern book are complete and accurate. We cannot, however, take responsibility for human error, typographical mistakes or variations in individual work.

ISBN: 978-1-59217-229-0
4 5 6 7 8 9

STAFF
Editor: Jeanne Stauffer
Managing Editor: Dianne Schmidt
Technical Artist: Kathy Wesley
Copy Supervisor: Michelle Beck
Copy Editors: Nicki Lehman, Judy Weatherford
Graphic Arts Supervisor: Ronda Bechinski

Graphic Artists: Pam Gregory, Erin Augsburger
Art Director: Brad Snow
Assistant Art Director: Nick Pierce
Photography Supervisor: Tammy Christian
Photography: Scott Campbell
Photo Stylist: Martha Coquat